God Is Enthralled By Your Beauty

Finally Looking Into The Mirror He Sees You In

TERESA ANN CRISWELL

TRIUMPHANT VICTORY PUBLISHING

Copyright © 2004, 2005, 2006, 2007, 2008, 2009, 2010, 2011, 2012, 2020, 2021, 2022
Teresa Ann Criswell

All rights reserved. Written permission must be secured from the publisher to use or reproduce any part of this book, except for brief quotations in critical reviews or articles.

Published in Winterset, IA

TRIUMPHANT VICTORY PUBLISHING
Library of Congress Registration Number TX 6-897-794

ISBN 9798609761019

Book Cover: *Canva*

Scripture quotations noted NKJV are from the NEW KING JAMES VERSION of the Bible. Copyright © 1979, 1980, 1982, Thomas Nelson, Inc., Publishers

Scripture quotations noted NASB are from the NEW AMERICAN STANDARD BIBLE®. Copyright © The Lockman Foundation 1960, 1962, 1963, 1968, 1971, 1972, 1973, 1975, 1977.
Used by permission.

Scripture quotations noted NIV are from the HOLY BIBLE: NEW INTERNATIONAL VERSION®. Copyright © 1973, 1978, 1984 by International Bible Society. Used by permission of Zondervan Publishing House. All rights reserved.

Scripture quotations noted AMP are from the THE AMPLIFIED BIBLE, Copyright © 1954, 1958, 1962, 1964, 1965, 1987 by the Lockman Foundation. All rights reserved.

Table of Contents

Dedication	04
Introduction	05
Chapter One What Mirror Do You See?	08
Chapter Two The Place of Secrecy	15
Chapter Three The King Adorned In Peace	21
Chapter Four The Eye of the Beholder	26
Chapter Five Beauty for Ashes	31
Chapter Six The Redeemer	37
Chapter Seven The Freedom Fighter	41
Thoughts from the Heart	50
Was This A Dream?	54
Knowing Jesus as Your Personal Lord and Savior	55
About The Author	58
Notes	61

DEDICATION

Lord, thank YOU for YOUR continual preparation, healing and deliverance over me as YOU are my Healer and Deliverer. I commit and dedicate this book to You, as I expect with great expectation that You will give it back blessed and anointed, setting your daughter's free, as each of us begin to know Who You truly are!

Also, to my precious parents, wonderful sisters and especially my earthly hero, my beloved husband Tim, my best friend and daughter Tristin, our son-in-love, Josiah and to my compassionate son Cody, amazing daughter in love, Jennifer and the pitter patter of my heart, my grandson, Nicholas Ray and granddaughter, Caroline Marie.

INTRODUCTION

The power of beauty seems to have disappeared and all that remains is the cloud of smoke that has sadly settled with perversion. The world's definition of beauty mutilates and destroys, as shallowness attempts to replace the true definition of depth.

This is a charge to all women, from the young to the elderly: we must know and realize the power of beauty and purity. The power of purity is not to be confused with timidity or fear; but beauty and purity of the Lord avails powerful strength; revealing who He is. We have tremendous responsibility to stand in our rightful place as daughters of the King. We must break down the walls of seclusion, insecurity, shame and masculinity disguised as feminism. We are not called to be men; we are called to be women of grace, executing righteousness (Lisa Bevere's book, *Fight Like a Girl*).

Imagine for a moment, looking into the loving eyes of God. Wow! To be overwhelmingly surprised as you begin to see who you truly are! His beautiful princess, His beautiful daughter, adorned in His amazing love, forgiveness, mercy, peace, gentleness and faithfulness as precious jewels adorn the crown upon our heads. Realizing we are clothed in the finest linen the world has ever seen; the linen of His grace. Our eyes filled with purity and gentleness.

Instead, many women look into the deceptive eyes of the enemy; clothed in torn, wrinkled, heavy garments of ugliness. The heavy coat of self-hatred, unforgiveness, judgment, anxiousness and depression was worn as the eyes of many are sadly filled with despair and hopelessness.

My beloved sister I believe that Jesus pleads with each of us and says, "No more my beautiful princess, I have delivered you from the lies of the enemy." In the Word of God, the Lord desires "...To give unto them beauty for ashes, the oil of joy for mourning, the garment of praise for the spirit of heaviness..."—Isaiah 61:3.

When reading this book, I believe you will find the journey of falling in love with the little girl you once knew and bring her forth to know her rightful place as a daughter of the King. We must allow other daughters, once and for all, to see the destructive and deceptive tactics of the enemy. It is a necessary mandate that they experience the transformation of God who is and reveals restoration and truth.

As you read this book, I pray you will allow Him to rescue you into His mighty arms of love and strength. More so, I pray you will only receive from this book what the Lord would have you to receive.

Finally, my great prayer of hope is that you choose to experience what is readily available to you; God's mighty power and majesty to overwhelm you with the great knowing that, "God is enthralled by your beauty" (Psalm 45:11).

Chapter One

What Mirror Do You See?

Definition of Mirror: 1: A polished or smooth surface (As of glass) that forms images by reflection
2: A true representation.

"For now we are looking in a mirror that gives only a dim (blurred) reflection [of reality as in a riddle or enigma], but then [when perfection comes] we shall see in reality and face to face! Now I know in part (imperfectly), but then I shall know and understand fully and clearly, even in the same manner as I have been fully and clearly known and understood [by God]."
1Corinthians 13:12 (Amp.)

I was enamored by the luxurious golden room filled with purity; draped with elegance and beauty.

Secretly I watched with delightful awe as this beautiful girl gazed across the room into her beautifully adorned mirror. She ran closer to the mirror with whimsical grace; seeing herself with amazement as the mirror revealed her magnificent beauty!

Incredibly awestruck, this beautiful little girl gazed into the mirror at the reflection of her beautifully shaped almond eyes. Her long lashes framed her piercing eyes; they fluttered gracefully as a butterfly. Stepping back with her fingers on her lips, she tilted her head to the side as if she heard a whisper. She smiled with assurance, and sighed with contentment, knowing who she was. She gracefully closed her eyes, leaning into hear the distinct and mighty whisper, which spoke dreams of romance.

The whisper led her into an incredible dance around the room; her dress spread open like a beautiful bell. It so perfectly twirled around as it suspended in the air. Her arms spread open, as her head tilted back; her long hair effortlessly tossed about as she freely danced to a song that I could not hear ~ only her ears could hear what seemed to be a beautiful melody. I found myself watching with envy, as she danced to a song ~ it would seem to be a song that has never graced our ears on earth, this song; only heard in heaven.

She danced with incredible freedom, an expression of her spirit taking flight as a soaring eagle. I was amazed by her knowing of who she was! She beheld the beauty of God and in seeing this, she was pleased.

I was so taken by the way she stared into the mirror. It was as though she could hear the distinct loving voice of her Father God. The music must have been the symphony of freedom. As I continued to watch in awe it would seem that she could hear her Daddy accompanying the „symphony of freedom" with His lyrics of beauty.

I realized with great astonishment that this little girl I secretly watched was none other than ~ me. I stood in disarray. I felt as if the ground and my body became one as I began to weep. I asked with a crying scream in disbelief, "Where did I go?" "What happened to me?"

Upon regaining my composure, I let out a cry of desperation. I found myself screaming for her and the only thing I could do was shout in great desperation with all that was within me, "Come back!" Yet it seemed my shouting only pushed her further away.

Suddenly, I awoke from what seemed like reality, gasping for air, I finally regained my breath.

Upon this awakening, I pondered the thought of being a child. It moved me as I realized many children seem to perceive the world through the eyes of purity. I must say that the reminiscing thought of being a small child was beyond an awakening, it was overflowing amazement.

The beautiful girl that I watched with incredible envy was truly blessed by her Father God. She saw the world she lived in with the eyes of a pure heart; the indescribable yearning and God given desire, to be free, loving, and to just be ~ His daughter and princess. She possessed a pure, loving heart that wanted to help every hurting person, every creature great and small. It was as though she lived her life looking into His mirror of beauty.

As she danced watching her reflection in the mirror; it was as though I could see her imaginations playing in her mind of herself dancing with the most handsome prince. Her dance revealed she had no doubt or question she was the most beautiful princess in all the land.

I then asked myself, "How did she come to this compelling realization that she was beautiful?" That is when I was lovingly reminded of the beautiful scripture in Psalm 139:14, "We are fearfully and wonderfully made." I ponder yet again; we are fearfully and wonderfully made.
Her display of gratitude and the graceful dance unto God revealed how our Father so beautifully placed this into our spirit.

Daughter, sister, mother, grandmother, friend...remember, you are fearfully and wonderfully made.

I realized with joy, that in the life of our once 3 year-old daughter, Tristin was absolutely in awe of herself. She was mesmerized by who she was. She looked into any mirror with confidence. It was as though I could see through those eyes of purity that she dreamed gigantic dreams. I remember when she would look into the mirror; or I should say, any mirror, she would turn her head slightly, placing her little hands on her hips and then naturally posing. She looked up at me with a serious, yet playful grin as her beautiful eyes pierced mine, wistfully asking in her small, yet high pitch voice, "What you think, Mom?" We giggled with each other and I had the opportunity to tell her that she was and still is the most beautiful little princess in the whole world.

Naturally, she looked up at me with her big, beautiful, brown eyes and said with incredible confidence, "Thank you!" She was glad that Mom agreed with what she already knew.

As I drifted back to sleep the same girl was before me in my dream. She was enchanted by this amazing, loving voice. Looking closer I realized, as tears streamed down my face, that as she looked into the beautifully adorned mirror, she was beholding The Eyes of her loving Father God and saw herself the way He saw her ~ with His grace and His beauty.

In an instant, faster than a suddenly moment, I saw something that did not make sense, yet I could not deny what I saw, for it was right before me.

There it was; a dark cloud moving in towards and over her. It was quickly approaching the room as it finally hovered over her. The cloud produced what would seem to be raindrops, yet, when I leaned into hear the rain fall, what I heard shocked me. I realized the rain fall was disguised with actual voices of the enemy influencing the world, repetitively chanting in an evil whisper, "You are not worthy." "You are ugly." "You have no beauty." "You are not important." "Shut Up! You have no voice."

I shouted at the voices, closing my ears not being able to bear one more voice of "death" spoken over her. I watched her as I prayed with great anticipation that she would ignore the deceptive voices. I had not yet seen her so scared until this very moment. She covered her head, shrinking into a position of helplessness.

To my dismay, this is when the unimaginable happened; she took her eyes off the beautifully adorned mirror and as though she was under a „spell", her eyes looked different, her beautiful smile ~ vanished. I grabbed hold of the floor as my nails clenched the ground, gritting my teeth in utter disgust and anger screaming, "They are lying to you! Don't listen to them! Look into the mirror!"

The voice that was so familiar, the voice of her Daddy, she felt overwhelmed and no longer looking into the mirror of beauty, she could no longer hear Him. As I watched in disbelief, the repetitive voices took over. She walked in unison and to the rhythm of the voices. She unknowingly walked over to the covered, uninviting object; so cold and overwhelmingly possessing utter depression.

She seemed to be in a trance and the eerie, evil voices subtly transformed from a whisper to a faint shout, as I heard, "Uncover it, uncover it..." Her hand slowly reached for the torn, aged fabric; old and tattered. The texture of the fabric was rough and heavy, somewhat comparable to an old, rough potato bag material. I could tell that the fabric had been used many times over. I pled with her, "Please! Listen and follow the voice of your Father God!"

Simultaneously as I pled with her, she slowly reached out her hand and uncovered the object. No! O God, No! What I saw was horrific! The girl that once danced to the song of beauty was now still. She was still with shock, looking into a glass object. This object looked like a mirror, but it was not. Her image, her reflection was distorted. She was so beautiful, yet the glass object revealed no beauty, the revealing object stripped her of what she truly was. She was looking into none other than the object of deception. The object was meant to kill her innocence, steal her purity and destroy her knowing of who she was.

When I saw her image all I could see was what she saw, and that was a girl who was battered, and full of despair. The evidence of life had been stripped from her eyes. The beautiful dress that she had been wearing was now violently replaced with torn and filthy rags.

Not only were my senses of what I saw overwhelming, but now the smell. The only thing I could compare the smell to is the smell of decay, revealing overwhelming sadness. The image was so familiar and then it „hit" me; this is when I believed the lie, versus continuing to believe the truth. To actually see at that very moment the devices and weapons of the enemy was utterly devastating.

Does this scene sound familiar? Is this you? Are you gripping your heart as it aches for this girl who has been deceived? Are you feeling a righteous indignation rise up within you as you realize that the beautifully adorned mirror, were as the loving eyes of God being rejected as she chose to see through the lies of the enemy. She chose the enemy's lie of bondage over the Truth of Freedom from her Father.

The mirror waits patiently for you to see what God sees. Are you looking into the loving eyes of God, or are you looking into the eyes of the enemy?

Awake, my sister! Awake! Hear the voice of your Father God!

"Arise [from the depression and prostration in which circumstances have kept you - rise to a new life]! Shine (be radiant with the glory of the Lord), for your light has come, and the glory of the Lord has risen upon you!"

~ Isaiah 60:1, AMP ~

Chapter Two

The Place of Secrecy

"Blessed (Happy, fortunate, to be envied) is he who has

forgiveness of his transgression continually exercised upon him, whose sin is covered. Blessed (Happy, fortunate, to be envied) is the man to whom the Lord imputes no iniquity and in whose spirit there is no deceit. When I kept silence [before I confessed], my bones wasted away through my groaning all the daylong. You are a hiding place for me; You, Lord, preserve me from trouble, you surround me with songs and shouts of deliverance. Selah [Pause and calmly think of that]! ~ Psalm 32:1-3, 7 (Amp.)

To watch her overwhelmed me with sadness. She stared at the distorted image of herself. Hopelessness annihilated her whole being.

I watched in disbelief as her weak, limp body convulsed like a rag doll as the lies of the enemy came at her like flying bullets. I watched her with painful compassion, as she seemed to be lifeless on the ground.

What I witnessed next was horrifying, right before my eyes I saw a treacherous leach-like creature, it slithered on the cold ground; about four feet in length and about six inches wide as it slowly crept onto her body. The creature had a name and it was called, *Bitterness*.

The manifestation of *Bitterness* was alarming. It literally changed and disfigured everything about her. The hope of that little girl that she once was, was now gone. It would seem as though there would be no trace of her again.

I painfully watched as this girl once full of life; whimpered with cries of hopeless regret. It seemed from the sounds of her cries that Bitterness was attaching itself to her in unimaginable pain. The eerie sound of her pain was overwhelming to my ears.

In the midst of the painful sounds of her cries, I heard her crying out, "Daddy"! "Daddy"! He immediately answered with a voice so booming and beautiful. Yet, even in His embracing voice, she did something that alarmed me and that was to ask a question that I could never bear to hear again, especially to ask such a question to the Father God. With a bitter tone and her fists clenched in anger, she yelled, "Why did you let this happen?"

The loud cry of bitterness was so painful. She inhaled deeply as if to cry even louder in between her cries and her breath. Then there was an excruciating, indescribable silence. The silence could be described as utter darkness to the ears. My ears had not experienced silence to this degree.

Crawling on the ground, I suddenly felt the ground shake below me, it shook with such power; it was God's Mighty tears falling to the ground.

Suddenly, I saw these two amazing hands. These hands were so beautiful. Hands so detailed with power. Hands I had never seen before as they tenderly took hold of her. His loving, booming voice said, "O my princess I am not to be judged. I am God and I cannot nor will not forsake any of my children."

She jumped angrily out of His unforgettable Hands without saying a word. However, her heart and eyes said it all as they filled with hate towards Him.

He stayed by her side as He whispered His promises, choking back loving tears. She drowned out His loving whisper by screaming and running into a room I had not yet seen until that very moment. The name above the door was posted a sign, "The Place of Secrecy." As she ran into the room, slamming the door behind her I could hear the tormenting screams.

In the midst of the screams, I suddenly heard a loud hammering sound. As I looked away, squinting my eyes afraid of what I might see, I placed my hands over my ears. Slowly opening my eyes, I could see in my peripheral vision the door slowly opening. Suddenly my sense of smell caught an odor that filled the air. The odor was unbearable. The only way to describe it was that it compared to that of a rotting corpse.

I was saddened to find that this girl that I once watched in amazement; this girl I once envied, I could hardly look upon, as sadness annihilated every part of me.

I realized in that moment that the unbearable odor which was so distinct, was the disturbing odor of what seemed to be unforgiveness. I saw it as an infectious wound that had never been treated, resulting in rottenness.

Curiosity captured me as the dream now placed me in "The Place of Secrecy." It was unbelievable what my eyes were seeing. Overwhelming fear overtook me as I sat trembling in her closet. Yet in that same moment, my eyes would not allow me to look away for I could not believe what I was seeing.

The images I saw can only be described as photographs. Many photographs sprawled about as they captured the painful moments of betrayal, lies, divorce, anger, unforgiveness, bitterness, grudges, unimaginable sins she had committed and sins that had committed against her.

Within the photographs, I could not see the faces as they had been carved out with what could have been a "knife of hate". These disturbing photographs that I saw before me cannot be articulated. The pictures of herself; they were pictures of self-inflicted wounds due to the overwhelming feeling of unworthiness.

Suddenly, the sense of touch below my feet caught me off guard as I realized I was standing in what I could only describe as warm goop. I slowly looked down with caution not knowing what I would see. As I looked down, I saw that beneath my feet I was standing in none other than her vomit. It was as if my two senses of touch and smell came together as one, causing great nausea.

The odor was unbearable; I would have to assume that when she opened the door to that place of secrecy, she was unable to open it alone. She hammered the images into this place of secrecy with her eyes shut. It would seem if she opened her eyes for a moment the images that were in this place were too much for even her stomach to bear.

Suddenly I disappeared from the scene and awoke in a cold sweat. The nightmare was so real and again so familiar. I asked God, "If it was too painful for her to see the images, why was she hammering those obscene images into this place of secrecy? Was this her way of punishing herself?"

I asked myself, "Are there things in my life that I have hidden that even I cannot bear to see on my own?" It came immediately to my spirit and the answer was, "Yes."

I found myself praying and pleading to God for this girl. I pled with unimaginable desperation, "Please open the door to the "Place of Secrecy" for her and even for me. This is a place of secrecy that she cannot bear to open herself!"

The pleading led me to ask myself, "Why is it that most daughters of God have chosen to look into this distorted object of what we think is a mirror?" "Why are we unknowingly drawn to ugliness versus beauty?"

I believe there are many issues, but the main natural reason is due to the deep wounds and ugly scars we have dared not look upon. Now why do we try to place those things into a place of secrecy? I believe it is not only survival mode, but also because we are made to believe it is better to ignore it and act as though it never happened, when in actuality it is as a festering poison in every area of our lives. There are wounds of guilt and unworthiness that must be revealed. Now please know what is revealed is not to be the focus, however, the focus is to give it to Your Rescuing Savior Jesus Christ so that He can be replace it with what God has so readily available for you ~ innocence and worthiness.

Our Daddy wants us to come to Him, no matter what we have done or have not done. He wants to lift us up, not to oppress us or be a victim of condemnation. We are His children. We are His daughters.

We as His daughters will not be able to bear the opening of that door without our Father's glorious love and grace. We must call upon Him!

I believe we will realize that this is not a bother to Him when we call upon Him. He wants us to call out to Him. He desires for us to know who we are in Him, but more than anything, He knows that we must know Who He is!

Chapter Three

The King Adorned In Peace

"Jesus straightened up and asked her, "Woman where are they? Has no one condemned you?" "No one, sir," she said. "Then neither do I condemn you," Jesus declared. "Go now and leave your life of sin."
~ John 8:10-11 (NIV)

I was swept back into this indescribable dream. As I watched her, I did not expect what would happen next. Her eyes did not blink as they were fixed to something with amazement! As her eyes were fixed, so mine became fixed upon the indescribable silhouette of a Man standing with great posture and stillness. However, this man was like no other. As He stood, He exuded great strength, He looked familiar and this man was in her room.

Walking closer to her, my eyes slowly gazed from the top of His head and down His amazing face. His head so beautifully graced with dark hair.

His amazing eyes filled with love. His chiseled jaw line as if He were carved out of a mountain. His lips so full as if I could see power sitting on the end of them. His neck thick and shoulders broad; defined as if the world sat upon them. His arms sculpted with strength and His hands scarred with gigantic scars, with amazing, indescribable power. His stature so tall, so mighty and becoming, I could not keep my eyes off of Him.

The world I was in seemed to stand still. Yet suddenly interrupted as my eyes were peeled from Him as I turned to look at her; she was frozen with shock.

The silence interrupted by her crackling voice as she softly asked, "Who are you?" He answered her with His powerful, deep, yet gentle, loving voice and said, "It is I, your King, and I am here to rescue you from the lies of bitterness, guilt, shame and unworthiness."

Hearing His voice caused me to tremble; His mighty voice sounded like many waves crashing against the sea. His voice filled with both authority and intense love. It was as though if He were to speak one more word, I would experience supernatural ecstasy. I longed for Him. I wanted Him like I wanted no other. I pled in secret for her to want Him; allowing Him to carry it all. I desired for her that He would be allowed to carry her out of this tormenting place of secrecy.

Suddenly, I jumped as I saw her jump with fear! She was not in fear of Him, yet she saw something, something I could not see, yet so painful that she actually turned her head from her King as if to say she was not good enough for Him. This thing she saw was none other than one of the enemy's greatest weapons of warfare; shame.

I saw her body fall to the ground as though she lost all the life left in her. Her limp body lying on the ground, and her face contorted in pain. Violently screaming, she placed her hands on her ears as if to stop the tormenting voices of condemnation only she could hear.

I pled for her to set her eyes upon and reach out to her King! This became intensely frustrating as she could not hear me, nor did she know that I was a groaning spectator, watching her in disbelief. Yet, The King waited patiently.

I watched this man with great intensity. He held her in His arms so ripped with strength, holding her seemingly lifeless body in His arms of indescribable, passionate strength. Her body convulsed violently as though she were being riddled by bullets of guilt. I was overwhelmed with sadness as I noticed that she was unaware that she was being passionately and lovingly held by this Mighty King of kings.

His lips so passionately pressed up against her tear stained cheeks. He wept over her weak body. It seemed hopeless. She believed the lie so deeply that her natural ear could only hear the lies of confusion. She came up off the floor; tearing herself away from this Mighty King and ran with shame, yet again, into The Place of Secrecy".

All I could do was scream with great pleading, hoping with great expectation that my desperate cries on her behalf would penetrate the invisible wall that separated her and I.

I cried out, "O God why is she so drawn to this place of secrecy?" Like an aerial view, I could see her room like I had not seen it before. I not only saw the distorted glass object, but I also saw the beautifully adorned mirror. I discovered that all she had to do was turn one hundred eighty degrees. If she chose to do this, I knew her eyes would be able to see clearly. She would once again see herself through the eyes of her Father.

I saw the mighty King standing as He interceded on her behalf. The way He prayed shook the foundations of this place with awesome power and majesty. It was as though the whole world had stopped. Time seemed to stop as I was swept away by His voice that spoke with such awesome authority. I had never heard any man speak with this kind of authority before. He was beyond confident. He was beyond valiant. He was amazing to watch. He was amazing to listen to.

Mesmerized by His valiant voice, I noticed as He walked silently to the door that opened to this place of secrecy. I sensed He was about to speak again and I leaned in with great anticipation. He slowly and gently opened the door and I heard Him say in a gentle yet strong whisper, "O my beloved, why do you choose to do this alone?"

What I saw next was nothing short of amazing! I saw a glimmer of hope in her eyes! She looked up to her King and with a sigh of great effort, she started to stand as she tightly grasped His amazing forearms and leaned into Him placing her head on His chest and with everything she had she desperately fell into Him. He with one hand caressed her face, lifting her head. She began to cry with what seemed like everything she had. Her whole body quivered as the inner cries poured out.

I was taken by surprise by His loving mercy over her. To hear Him cry over her was so heart wrenching and I realized His passionate love for her. He knew who she was to become. He saw her through eyes of beauty. Watching Him hold her was so pure, yet it took my breath away. His mighty arms so defined; engulfing her whole being.

It was the most powerful scene to watch Him hold her; seeing restoration revealed right before my eyes. The restoration came upon her head, her eyes, and her heart and all the way down to the soles of her feet. The girl I once watched with amazement is literally being restored right before my eyes.

The Kings hands embraced her face as His hands held her blushing cheeks. His loving hands removing the dirt and tears off her beautiful face. He ran His hands so gently through her hair. She looked into His eyes and He looks into hers. As if time had stopped; He brought her close and placed His beautiful lips upon her forehead. Miraculously, this glorious light from His presence engulfed her being and I saw this miraculous transformation.

At the power of this transformation; I heard evil screams come forth. However, the screams were not of her. They were the screams of the voices of guilt, bitterness, shame and unworthiness that had no chance in the presence of the King! King Jesus!

I watched with joy as I saw her turn with the King and she finally looked into the beautifully adorned mirror. As she looked she was stunned to see her new image. Her eyes now filled with freedom.

He slowly arose and lovingly reached out His hands to hers. She had a glorious, beaming smile upon her face.

Then, I awoke...

Chapter Four

The Eye of the Beholder

"...I am fearfully and wonderfully made..."-Psalm 139:14

I awoke to a memory.

Just as the little girl in the beginning, so I was. I knew how beautiful I was. Yet, the devastating memorable moment when it all changed, the moment I entered my kindergarten class.

The mirror I looked into was shattered. I looked into the distorted object which reflected the hurtful insults. It seemed like a true mirror, but it wasn't. My peers did not see beauty in me and in turn I allowed them to become the "eye of the beholder" in my life.

I must say, I remembered that day so vividly. The transition was unfair, for I was a princess at home, yet when coming to school for the first time, I was suddenly different. I did not realize how different until that very moment.

I remember the first insult that was hurled at me, as they pointed their fingers, and crinkling their noses,

"Ewwwwww, Chinese." As the kids said it, they pulled their eyes in a slanted position and laughed. I remembered desperately wanting to run out of that place.

Almost immediately I allowed that day to mold me into an insecure, resentful young girl. I began resenting my own mother who is a beautiful Korean woman and thinking to myself, "I'm made fun of because of her. I wish I looked like the other girls. They have light hair and light eyes and they aren't made fun of." I remember wanting to be of no part of my culture whatsoever. I thought to myself, "My mom ruined my life." Of course, that was a lie, but this is what started forming in my little mind.

I could no longer hear the compliments of the people who loved me and whom I loved, for I did not hear confirmations outside the home; I only heard the opposite. I was focused on the negative insults hurled at me almost daily as a little girl. I fought back with mean words, which did not help my situation or anyone else's. Of course as a child, this was and is hard to comprehend.

So, I interrupt this memory and ask you a question...who is the "eye of the beholder" in your life? Is it you, your peers, your spouse? Or is it Almighty God, the One who created you? If the eye of the beholder is you, then this could be a detriment if what you see is of despair. I believe this issue alone affects our relationships with our family, spouse and sadly enough even our own children.

We need to step back, wake up and pay attention to what we are saying about ourselves; especially when in the presence of our children.
We need to listen to ourselves and know that our children observe our self-destructive comments and will most likely

turn on the heels of the lie we have spoken over ourselves and believe it for themselves.

Our children are so much more aware of life than we give them credit for. So many times they are aware and sensitive to our feelings, more so than we are. They will often wonder, "Why is mom sad?" "Why is mom upset?" "Did I do something to make mom feel that way"?

The negative words we speak over our lives, we have received as gifts, when they were not intended to be received at all (Proverbs 18:21).

Who knew that the enemy would not have to use his own weaponry...but we, ourselves, could commit self-sabotage on our own lives to demoralize and even defame who God says we are.

Have you ever heard yourself talk about who you are as a person? I have caught myself cut down on many areas of who I am and in turn defame the person in whom God created.

We have actually believed that we have a „right" to say these awful things about ourselves. What and who gave us this right? It is not God, because we are to live our life to glorify Him. How does it glorify God when we say the opposite of what He says about us?

It is evidently clear that this does not glorify God because with our words and actions we say with great ignorance that The King of kings ultimately made a mistake; which we know ~ He cannot lie nor does He have the ability to make mistakes (Numbers 23:19).

As it so eloquently is recorded in Isaiah 29:16 (New Living Translation), "How stupid can you be? He is the Potter, and he is certainly greater than you. You are only the jars he makes! Should the thing that was created say to the one who made it, "He didn't make us"? Does a jar ever say, "The potter who made me is stupid"?"

When I read this scripture, I was astounded at the same accusation I unknowingly had towards God. Me, being the clay, judging God, the Potter, as if to say He knows nothing about what I am, when He is, The Great I Am!

Isn't it amazing how we think we have it all figured out? God is so merciful, no wonder he says, "My mercy is new every morning" (Lamentations 3:22-23). The mercy He has over us is actually for Himself, we become beneficiaries of that mercy as He is so patient over us.

Are you ready to live a life of True Freedom in Christ Jesus? It is readily available. Are we willing to fix our eyes upon the beautifully adorned mirror? If so, God, the Creator of the heavens and the earth is so lovingly, I would presume sighing with relief as The Great I Am says of you, "You have finally believed what I have said of you all along. My beautiful princess, you are adorned in My radiant love over you; for I Am enthralled by your beauty, you have finally looked into the mirror I see you in."

(Referencing, Psalm 45:10 & 11).

You might even ask, "Why do you keep emphasizing beauty?" I believe it is the core of God's creation throughout the earth. He is the Author of True Beauty. I keep emphasizing beauty because it is emphasized every day in front of our eyes wherever we go. However, the beauty that we have been exposed to has been through the impure, sadistic ways of the world.

Personally, I lived a life of "please approve of me." I would conform to anything you wanted, sadly, no matter the cost. If it cost my family, okay, as long as you accept me. It was a sad and misconstrued way of living and I lived it.

In fact, I would not call it living, but existing as a life with absolutely no purpose. I didn't live on purpose, I lived as though every choice I made was an accident. I lived a life of looking into the mirror and not realizing that there I stared into the eyes of a precious spirit whom God fearfully and wonderfully made (Psalm 139).

When your eyes meet your reflection in the mirror, do you catch a glimpse of a precious jewel that the world does not yet know about? As you look into the mirror do you see a glimmer of hope? Do you see a woman who has filled herself up with lies and now realizes that it is about time she knows the truth?

What is the truth? You are a woman of strength and might. Your Father is the King of kings. He with passion and pleasure lets the kingdom know that you are His daughter. He bids you to come so that the world may see what has been violently kidnapped from them. You have something that they never knew they needed until they laid eyes upon you. There is something inside you from the Lord that must get out! Your gift is not to be hoarded, but to be graciously received by others.

God desires to deliver us from living the counterfeit and delivering us into the life we were meant to live; the life of authenticity. The revealing mandate of His majestically glorious beauty!

Chapter Five

Beauty for Ashes

Definition of Beauty: 1: The quality present in a thing or person that gives intense pleasure or deep satisfaction to the mind, whether arising from sensory manifestations (as shape, color, sound, etc.), a meaningful design or pattern, or something else (as a personality in which high spiritual qualities are manifest).

Definition of Ashes: 4: ashes, deathlike grayness; extreme pallor suggestive of death. Ruins, esp. the residue of something destroyed; remains; vestiges; the ashes of their love; the ashes of the past. Mortal remains, esp. the physical or corporeal body as liable to decay. Anything as an act, gesture, speech, or a feeling, that is symbolic of penance, regret, remorse or the like.

As I fell asleep, I drifted into a beautiful dream. I suddenly appeared in the most unforgettable valley with sculpting, cascading mountains all around me. I took notice of the beautiful, breathtaking trees, their height so grand; their green leaves so vibrant with color. The smells, the color and especially the scenery were overwhelmingly real. I watched the rushing, translucent waters brilliantly flowing over rocks bending into streams and rivers. I could hear the sound of a violently rushing, beautiful river to the distance and the picturesque sound of an amazing waterfall crashing upon the waters below.

The beauty was intoxicating for all my senses. The smells and scenery were so crisp with effervescent life.

As I stood in amazement, suddenly the thought of the unforgettable girl came to my mind. I wondered, "Where is she?" I knew I was to find her to see what she had become. As soon as I had the thought of her, I saw a beautiful silhouette of a woman off to the distance. She looked remarkable, she had transformed from a feeble, insecure girl; filled with shame, into an elegant, incredibly beautiful woman.

I noticed she was barefoot and twirling about in the meadow; the grass somewhat high as I saw each twirling step she took and at the same time I could hear the sound of grass crunching beneath her feet. She was humming a joyful sound.

Her long beautiful hair tossed so freely around her face and along her back as she aimlessly sang and danced. The golden highlights pierced through her dark brown hair as the sunlight shone upon her head.

Off to the distance, I saw the beautiful animals from the mountains curiously coming out, watching her in wonder. Their ears perked up as they were still with awe. It was so cute to watch their heads move ever so slightly as if they were puzzled. When I came closer to where she was, I saw what looked like dirt flying out of her hands as she twirled about. She released what looked like ashes into the wind for it seemed she knew something miraculous was about to happen.

As she twirled about, I saw the smile upon her beautiful face, her teeth glistening white as she effortlessly spun around and floated about like a feather. She was stunning to watch. I marveled and I watched her dance to a sound of freedom. It was as if the whole world had disappeared and it was just her and her Father God. Her hair swung about her face, bouncing back and forth upon her shoulders, caressing her back. I loved watching her as she ran with her hands down by her side as they glided along the long blades of grass. She tumbled and rolled onto the ground; giggling with relief. Suddenly still, she laid there on the ground, closing her eyes, basking in the warm sun as she looked up with a smile of contentment at the clear blue sky.

As she opened her mouth to speak, it sounded like a song, a beautiful melody of freedom and joy. Her voice so softly and gently spoke to God. She spoke so softly to Him as though He were lying next to her holding her hand. She giggled as a little girl curled up in safety as though she was next to her Daddy. She said in a child-like voice, "I love you God."

I could see the splendor of His Peace come over her as she turned over on her side and curled up into a ball. With grace and peace, she fell asleep. She was a woman of intriguing beauty.

As she slept...I awoke to reality. I yearned to dance like she did. In my pajamas I eagerly jumped out of bed with excitement, as a little girl, I began to twirl. As I twirled about, I giggled and looked up, remembering the freedom at that moment from when I was a child. I looked down at the carpeted floor below my feet, twirling some more, and the area that I twirled in seemed to turn into a giant "cinnamon roll". The joy came over me as I giggled in dizziness. As I twirled, for that moment, all the cares and worries literally „flew" away from my consciousness. This expression allowed me to come to God as a little princess knowing, without doubt, who my King was.

I reminisce of the dream and realized that God so passionately took every evil, vile thing that she gave to Him and He dissolved it with His amazing, glorious Love. His presence, His All- Consuming Fire of Love burned it up and caused it to cease from existence in her life. She may have a memory of it but the pain and sting of that memory ceased all together.

I am so enveloped by the recollection of the dream that I became caught up in another vision. Immediately I was startled as I heard what sounded like trumpets sounding from heaven. I spun around quickly as I heard the sound of horse's hoofs and suddenly, I saw the Mighty Man of Valor, The King adorned in Peace who came towards me down from the mountains, it was Jesus!

As I saw Him approaching, I just knew that He was coming for her, when to my surprise He stopped right before me and He smiled. Oh his smile melted me in my place as I stared into the most loving eyes I had ever seen. His eyes filled with purity, vast as the sky, so pure and eternal, His unforgettable eyes painting a picture with me in it.

He reached out to me with His Arm of Salvation as I grabbed hold of Him. With overwhelming strength He swung me up and around to ride behind Him on His beautiful white stag. There was nothing I could say but hold on to Him as He galloped away with me embracing Him. All I knew was I did not want to let go of Him. It wasn't that I didn't want to let go because of the fear of falling; I didn't want to let go because of Who I was holding onto. The only thing I could do at this moment as my face pressed against His strong back was to embrace Him. I could smell His amazing fragrance. The fragrances were so lovely, the lily of the valley and the rose of Sharon.

I have smelled many beautiful fragrances but His fragrant odor was heavenly, peaceful and strong.

I was captivated by His fragrance and realized with awe that I was getting to ride with none other than the King of kings. It would seem that the blades of grass, the trees, the animals and waters were bowing down to Him as we galloped by. His presence annihilated everything with His love; I thought to myself, "How could I for one moment ever stress about who I am ever again"? "I know who I am because I am starting to know who He truly is."

When I rode with Him, I knew that I was important; I knew that I was beautiful. As I heard the words come out of His mouth, it would seem as if the whole world stopped to hear this Voice that could never be mimicked. For His voice was of love and compassion accompanied with authority and strength. In awe, I heard Him say, "Do you know how I long for you?" This question not only startled me but it also paralyzed me as I was in awe to hear such words come out of His amazing mouth. This mind-blowing thought, "You long for me?" At that moment, I knew the answer was "yes" for the answer was revealed as I was in His glorious presence.

His presence was like a heartbeat that pulsated with unfailing love. Worthiness was what he crowned upon my head and then placed around my neck the jewels of wisdom and understanding. When I felt His hands caress my neck it caused me to want Him even more. The realization of who was with me, I became weak, becoming obsessed with Him. I found myself wanting only Him; nothing else and no one else.

No wonder the girl twirled about and lay freely on the ground so sure of who she was. Jesus, The King adorned in peace, rescued her.

I then realized this desperate obsession I had for Him was only a glimpse of how He longs to be in continual fellowship with us. His love for you and for me has consumed and annihilated the shame, regrets, unforgiveness, bitterness, hatred and grudges we have embraced long enough and He has replaced it with His glorious beauty of redemption and restoration.

Will you allow His beauty upon your life?

Chapter Six

My Redeemer

Definition of Redeemer: 1: He recovers by discharging an obligation 2: To free or rescue by paying a price 3: To free from the consequences of sin 4: To remove the obligation of by payment also: to convert into something of value 5: To make good by performing: fulfill 6: To atone for

"For I know my Redeemer and Vindicator lives, and at last He [The Last One] will stand upon the earth." Job 19:25 AMP

King Jesus led me by the hand as we walked together.

The moon illuminated the dark, starlit sky, yet with a haze of smoke coming forth from the distance, everything around me was intensified. As I heard the leaves rustling together in the wind, I was drawn to this beautiful mountain, when I heard my King Jesus say, "Do you want to see the amazing sight over this hill?" With excitement, I said, "Yes, King Jesus! Wherever you go, I want to go!"

As we ran together, the night wind passed through my hair and at that moment I felt as though the whole world was in slow motion, experiencing peace annihilate every part of my being. When we reached the incredible scene, I realized where the smoke was coming from. It was an amazing bonfire. I was surprised to see such a huge fire with only one person. There she stood, a beautiful woman. Jesus drew me near as He whispered, "Watch and see her need be fulfilled." I intently watched Him walk over to her as I stood off to the distance. My curiosity of what He would do next, drew me closer. As I drew closer, I realized it was her; the girl who I saw in my dreams. There she stood before the bonfire emptying the contents of a box that was simply labeled "lies".

It was amazing as I watched, to know that as she emptied this box of „lies" the One who stood beside her was Truth!

She looked to her side and realized that Jesus her King stood beside her. As tears streamed down her fire lit cheeks, she started to shake as tears welled up within her innermost parts. She slowly handed the box over to Jesus. I watched Him gently grasp one of her hands as He so beautifully accepted the box with His other hand. To hear His gigantic, gorgeous whisper I heard Him say, "You are ready, you can do this, I Am with you."

Together they emptied the contents of this box into the fire. He did something incredibly amazing. He not only emptied the box but He threw the box itself into the fire. Right before my eyes, I saw the „scales" literally be removed from her eyes. It was not just one layer but it seemed to be layer after layer. As the scales came off, her countenance changed right before my eyes. It was as though I could see the thoughts going through her mind. They seemed to be thoughts of peace and new territories of freedom that she dared even dream existed. She sat down with her legs criss-crossed as she sat on the ground and her arms rested on the side of her knees as she made sure that the contents of the box and the box itself were truly being consumed never to return.

It seemed like an eternity as she stared into the dimming, crackling fire. She finally spoke to Jesus. She said, "How could I have left you Lord? Thank you for Your forgiveness over me for living a life as if to say, there was something better than You."

With regret in her voice, she said, "Where would I have been if only, I had been with you?" As Jesus the King sat with her, He so passionately touched the tip of her chin and softly lifted her head that seemed to hang in shame. He lifted her head, as tears streamed down her face. He said, "If you would have stayed with Me all those years you would be right where you are."

When I heard those words spoken to her, I was still with awe. I thought, "Wait! So that is what it is! Redemption! It is truly an active experience as the Redeeming power of God came upon her." He was truly The Redeemer. He turned those ashes into beauty. I believed when He said, "You would be right where you are" I don't believe He meant in the literal sense of this dimension of time, however I believe He meant her heart's desire was now for Him, right where it needed to be; where her heart was destined to remain.

I now ask you, "Can you see her?" "Can you see the tiara upon her head?" "Do you see her looking into the eyes of God?" "Can you see her dancing?" "Can you see her smiling?" "Can you finally see her pleased with who she is?" "As you see her, do you see yourself?"

You must know by now that He is holding you with arms of unfailing love! He with incredible desire, longs to lavish you with His loving faithfulness which is higher than the highest mountain. His love is deeper than the deepest sea even more than all the bodies of water on this earth put together.

He redeems you from what you could not and cannot become on your own.

What is it about Him that can change your perspective of yourself in one life altering moment? The life changing perspective is because of His love. His Love is an "All-Consuming Fire" that burns and disintegrates the lies.

Do you see His loving hands extended out to you? I plead with you! Take His Mighty Hands. "He will lead you to paths of life." "He will make those crooked paths straight" (Psalm 16:11, Isaiah 42:16).

When adversity comes, why go through it alone? He conquered adversity, which makes you more than a conqueror...you get to go through it with Him knowing what waits for you on the other side...Victory!

Go to the fire with King Jesus and allow Him to burn that cloak of lies that have been deceptively hemmed together with bitterness, unworthiness, unforgiveness, hate and strife. Watch what He does with the ashes of that cloak...be amazed by what only He can do...REDEEM!

Chapter Seven

The Freedom Fighter

"Yes, furthermore, I count everything as loss compared to the possession of the priceless privilege (the overwhelming preciousness, the surpassing worth, and supreme advantage of knowing Christ Jesus my Lord and of progressively becoming more deeply and intimately acquainted with Him [of perceiving and recognizing and understanding Him more fully and clearly]. For His sake I have lost everything and consider it all to be mere rubbish (refuse, dregs), in order that I may win (gain) Christ (the Anointed One). And that I may [actually] be found and known as in Him, not having any [self-achieved] righteousness that can be called my own, based on my obedience to the Law's demands (ritualistic uprightness and supposed right standing with God thus acquired), but possessing that [genuine righteousness] which comes through faith in Christ (the Anointed One), the [truly] right standing with God, which comes from God by [saving] faith."
-Philippians 3:8-9

Definition of Know: 1:To perceive directly: have understanding or direct cognition of: also: to recognize the nature of 2: To be acquainted or familiar with 3: To be aware of the truth of 4: To have a practical understanding of

Now imagine for a moment, you are on the beach. You can hear the waves and the sound effects of the wind. If you are wearing pants, roll them up and walk towards the beach ~ sit down and let your toes dig into the wet sand ~ listen to the sounds of the seagulls off to the distance.

Are your senses mesmerized by the symphony of the wind and waves as they crash together and become one? It may be the most beautiful symphonic arrangement to your ears. Just stand there and let the vastness of the ocean and the breeze of the wind caress your face and hair as the tide comes in so smoothly and brushes up against your feet and above your ankles. Slowly inhale that beautiful fresh ocean air... now slowly exhale. Open your eyes and look into the horizon, look to the left and now to the right...there seems to be no end to this splendid ocean as it seems to go on for eternity.

Awake my sister, God's love is more vast than all the grains of sand in the entire world.

Ponder this thought for a moment: you are on the beach looking out to the horizon, that one area where you are standing look to your right, now look to your left, now look straight ahead. You cannot see the end of the ocean; it keeps going even beyond what your eyes can see!

Wow! Now listen to the rhythm of the waves crashing in. Listen to that ongoing sound; the sound of power. Now, imagine your head upon God's Almighty chest and that sound of the rhythm of the waves is as His Awesome heartbeat.

O Princess, He wants you to know His love is more than enough! More than your parents love, your husband's love, your children's love, your friend's love all put together does not come close to God's enthralling love for you! His capacity to love is so great, for this is Who He Is. God Is LOVE!

Obviously, we will never understand the vastness of who He is, but let us consider a few amazing characteristics of

God. Well, most of us have been taught according to the Word that He is "The Great I Am". He is "All Sufficient". He is "The Redeemer". He Is "The King of kings". He is "The Lord of lords". He is our "Provider". He is "More Than Enough". He is "The Commander of The Heavenly Hosts". He "Reigns In Victory". "He is Love". He is "The Beginning and The End". "He made all things and for Him they were made". He is our "Strong Tower". He is our "Refuge". He is our "Redeemer" - The many words to give descriptions of adoration in Who He is, is definitely eternal. The amazing truth is that these describe only a glimpse of Who He is. These descriptive, active words are not clichés that we often times use loosely. These words reflect the attempting power of letters forming words to collaborate such emphasis to worship Him. Vocabulary itself cannot contain such massive power!

In this massive power, He imparts Who He is...and that is Freedom revealed because of Truth! God has so freely and lavishly given us freedom. He has given us the keys to see ourselves through His loving, beautiful, merciful eyes. He has given us the ability to run from the lies with His powerful grace as we run with great humbleness to Him, The Truth.

In humbleness, we will find that we will no longer dwell on the actions of how people have wronged us. For we realize that when we focus on people, we lead ourselves right back into captivity. When we look to God and lean on Him the One who cannot fail, we stay in that place of BEING free.

Knowing that Jesus is most powerfully the Key to freedom, how do we come to this realization? It is by the Spirit of God revealing The Word, Jesus Christ, as we get to know Him and His character through what He has already done and continues to do as revealed in scripture.

As I read through the gospels, the writers have a common thread that is so beautifully knit together. As Jesus performed miracles, there was this genuine, authentic, wondrous, uncontainable love that was lavished upon the unlovable. Jesus repeatedly gave glory to the Father as He would say, "I do this because I have first seen my Father in heaven do this." We also know that He had compassion and intimacy with His Father on earth as flesh. He knew who He was, yet He also knew that in order to do the great exploits that we triumphantly read about, Jesus knew He had to be dependent upon the Father. His power was manifested by His humble dependency on God's compassion.

The dependency on The Father is incredibly amazing. However, I am brought to this glorious reminder of Who Jesus is revealed as Truth. Paul, the apostle had such a revelation of Jesus, revealing an active, vivid picture of the Armor of God.

I want to bring focus on the belt of Truth. This belt girds us about. Jesus is that belt of truth that girds us about as one of the pieces of spiritual armor (Ephesians 6:10-18). He girds us, He holds us in who He is and what He does.

The definition of gird according to Webster's Dictionary:

1. To encircle or fasten with or as if with a belt (on a sword).
2. To invest especially with power or authority.
3. To prepare or brace.

Watch! Listen! See this!
Jesus encircles us or fastens us with His truth (The Word of God is as the sword).
He invests in us with power and authority.

He prepares us and braces us with His love.
He not only frees us he also equips us in His authority on how to remain in that place, by being embraced by Him.

Now it is our choice to stay in that powerful, loving embrace or walk away from it and go directly back into the deceitful lies of captivity.

> "In [this] freedom Christ had made us free [and completely liberated us]; stand fast then, and do not be hampered and held ensnared and submit again to a yoke of slavery [which you have once put off].
>
> –Galatians 5:1 AMP

I'll give you an example. I was meditating on an illustration that God had given to me, in regards to how He is the key to freedom. His name; Jesus, is the Key. He broke me free from the bondage of my past that I constantly dwelt upon. He showed me that when I was set free, He would say with excitement, "Teresa, you are free from this prison of captivity, now Come to Me!" In this visual I watched myself only standing in the cell, not coming out. I thought for sure I would run out of the prison shouting and rejoicing; embracing my Mighty Rescuer, Jesus. But to my dismay, instead, I felt the indentations of the cuffs that once held me by my wrists and ankles, and it was as if I had that feeling of "forgetting my jewelry" wanting to go back and put it back on. I lived a life of captivity for so long, that I was unable to experience freedom, for the familiarity of captivity held me back in the demented comfort of the chains. This time without the adversary's help, I placed those chains of the past back upon myself.

This powerful illustration shocked me. I remember crying out to God, "Why would I do such a thing?" "Why do I deny your power not with my words but with my actions?" It is as if I heard the Spirit of God say, "The Israelites did the same, reliving a false, demented memory of the past."

They forgot how awful it was being in captivity, they had a false memory in the heat of the moment of "how much better Egypt was" than where they were. Of course, they were in the wilderness, not a place anyone wants to be, however they weren't alone. They had Almighty Jehovah parting the Red Sea so they could cross over from the land of captivity into the land of promise and freedom. Almighty God was their "Cloud by day" and "Fire by night". He provided manna from heaven and when they were complaining of how tired they were of eating bread from heaven, and how they wanted meat. So, God in His abundant provision, provided quail, but not just enough quail, there was so much quail it went for a couple of miles and stacked waist deep.

There were many impossible situations, yet, the God of the impossible would make it possible. Anytime I read those historical accounts of the Israelites, I ask God with great frustration, "How could they forget what You, Almighty God had done?" Yet, sadly I was reminded that I do the same thing!

When I saw the imagery of the Israelites, I shook my head in sadness for what an awful attempt to unintentionally judge God by attempting to slap God's Holy face. The Deliverer was being told by the ones who were delivered that He did not do a good enough job for their sakes. The astonishing part, they only knew slavery, the only life they ever knew. For more than four hundred years they were in captivity, so being free was absolutely foreign.

They were free but still had a slavery mentality. The spirit of slavery, blinded them from seeing the beauty of freedom that they stood in.

I no longer want to be guilty of having a slavery mentality. I no longer want to be guilty of having an oppressive mentality, to reject freedom because I have no idea what it is, most likely because I have forgotten Who He truly is!

This is such an awakening. I must know my God, The God who Frees and Restores back to us what we may have never known before...a free woman.

I have heard it said, "Your past does not determine your future." I believe that to some degree, however, most people's past does determine their future by wrong choices. So in this, I choose to say, "Your past does not have to determine your future."

We must make choices every moment of the day. One of those choices, revealed by these questions, "Will I allow yesterday's failures and decisions determine today"? Of course, we want to say, "No!" But how do we live that out?

I believe with some of us we have to remind ourselves literally every moment of the day by speaking aloud, declaring with a SHOUT into the atmosphere over ourselves:

"I am Free."
"I am set free!"
"I am disentangled from lies!"
"I am relieved and cleared by Jesus!"

We must shout and declare it with a shout of praise unto God with great fervency!

To the degree that slavery has tried to come after us is to the degree we must resist it! How? By submitting to and trusting in God.

We unwillingly told ourselves how we could never be free, so we now must be willing to echo what is truth... "I am free, because of my Freedom Fighter, Jesus Christ!"

Think about this. Unwillingly we tend to live our lives as a lie...when willingly we must live Truth.

With freedom, we must uphold it.

We maintain that freedom by maintaining intimate time with the Author of Freedom. For when the will goes away to be intimate with the Freedom Fighter, then the unwillingness will sneak back in and will snatch us with its clenching jaws as we become a slave to the lies, yet again.

Willingness comes at a price. However, the incredible, awesome outcome is freedom and truth!

We must also remember that unwillingness comes at a price for the results are lies and destruction, which does not reveal the glory of God.

Which will we choose? I pray we will say "Yes" to the King and live as our rightful place in His Glorious Kingdom as daughters of Truth!

You have lived the life of peasantry long enough...you have a legacy to leave...be a part of rescuing the little girl from the lies of the enemy and experience the Redeeming power to change the outcome of her life by living the life of freedom!

Remember, this is more than a daily walk. This is moment by moment. This is a life of choices; those choices not only remain with you but they will and can remain with the generations after you. If you have an unwillingness to do it for yourself, then be a visionary and do it for the generations after you that you do not hear!

Realize that they are crying out for someone to make the right choices for God's glory. Walk the path of His glory. You are not a peasant; you are His daughter! You are no longer an orphan; you are His royal heiress!

I plead with you! Look into the mirror and see the daughter of the King! Rise up, for remember, God is enthralled by your beauty.

Thoughts from the Heart

What are some qualities that give pleasure to your senses? I remember living in Utah and every morning waking up to the beautiful mountains from our master bedroom. It was not just awaking to the picturesque mountains, but the scenery from the valley was captivating. It was so wondrous that my eyes were able to see and experience such great magnificence every single morning. The humbling experience was like watching a priceless painting come to life.

The peaks of the mountains were adorned in white and clothed in luscious green trees; they were accompanied by the crisp blue sky as though the sky were the mountains shawl.

As I give this detailed description of the scenery, I believe God loves and created the details within us for His great pleasure. We get to enjoy the beauty He graciously placed upon us. He did it for His pleasure, and we are beneficiaries of such beauty.

Think on beauty for a moment. Have you ever noticed that when you see a person, a place or an object of beauty, you unknowingly become disengaged from everything around you and stare? I have found myself staring at such beauty. I dare to wonder if God, Who created all things whether it is the person He created or the object that was made by the person He created, how He must be intoxicated with us. I would dare to believe that He stares at us with such pleasure knowing He did good.

I want to go deeper than that. He beholds you with His unfailing love and only sees beauty. Your beauty enthralls Him. I am sure that even the heavens boom with His excitement as He looks upon you. I believe that God is so in love with you and the beauty He places upon you is so powerful, if He were to speak to you He would describe such beauty that your ears have never heard. You would hear majestic beauty with such adjectives in which all the languages put together could not translate. I believe that our mind would not be able to comprehend such array of words from the Almighty Father God upon our lives!

I like to imagine this is what he says of you, "O My masterpiece of beauty. You are a reminder to Me that I am amazing. You are more beautiful than all the oceans and waves of every size, depth and curl put together. The mountains of the world do not compare to the beauty I see in you. Yes, you are My masterpiece and no philanthropist, nor the wealthiest man in the entire world would be able to afford such priceless treasure as you. However, you have prostituted yourself as a worthless object when I have called and graced you to be much more than even royalty. I have crowned you with jewels that the earth's soil has never dared to touch. If you knew the value upon your head, you would live a life of abundance that even the wealthiest of the wealthiest would envy you. Every piece of sand upon the earth if all accounted for, still does not describe your worth."

This beautiful reminder takes me to Song of Solomon as The Beloved (I believe could represent Jesus) speaks to The Shulamite (Could represent us). These are the wonderful words He speaks to her, imagine him saying this to you: *"If you do not know, O fairest among women...your cheeks are lovely with ornaments, your neck with chains of gold. Behold, you are fair, my love! Behold, you are fair! You have dove eyes. I am the rose of Sharon, and the lily of valleys. Like a lily among thorns, and the lily of the valleys."*

"The Beloved then brings her to the banqueting house, and his banner of her is love. His left hand is under her head, and his right hand embraces her. He leaps upon mountains, skipping upon the hills. He is like a gazelle or a young stag." "Behold, he stands behind our wall; He is looking through the windows, gazing through the lattice." He then speaks to her and says, "Rise up, my love, my fair one, and come away. For lo, the winter is past, the rain is over and gone. The flowers appear on the earth; the time of singing has come. And the voice of the turtledove is heard in our land. The fig tree puts forth her green figs, and the vines with the tender grapes give a good smell. Rise up, my love, my fair one, and come away! O my dove, in the clefts of the rock, in the secret places of the cliff, let me see your face, let me hear your voice; for your voice is sweet, and your face is lovely."

She hesitates and lingers as he calls for her, she then seeks Him and He is not to be found. As I picture this, I can see that she panics in want for Him she then says to herself, "I will arise now," she goes about the city, she goes to the streets and in the squares she is saying to herself that she will seek the one she loves. She seeks him but does not find him. The watchmen who go about the city find her and I can see her with tears of panic as she screams, "Have you seen the one I love?" At that moment, I imagine her Beloved watching her through the lattice and seeing how long she will seek for Him. He wonders, "Will she seek me for a while then hurry back to her life." "Will she seek me until she finds me?" He watches her I believe hoping that she chooses to seek Him until she finds Him. Then, I picture the men mocking her as they see what seems to be a crazy woman in the middle of the night, most likely drunk with wine. Finally, after looking for Him and not giving up she finds Him and as she finds Him she runs to Him and embraces Him and will not let Him go.

What a whirlwind!

I have asked myself if I desire and want Him with everything I have? Have I ever sought Him so passionately that I dropped everything in life and searched Him out as though I were searching for treasures of gold? I want to go beyond what even the Shulamite woman did, I want to arise when He tells me to arise, I want to go to Him while He still may be found. I do not want to delay in my obedience unto Him.

I pray that you will allow the Lord to bless you for He wants to lavish you with His love; for He is enthralled by your beauty (Psalm 45:10 & 11).

Was This A Dream?

Many have asked, "Teresa, did you have these dreams?" The answer is "No." What was written did not consist of dreams. The writings conveyed in this book were more of a vision that was laid out before me as I wrote. During the writing process of this book, it became a journey of imageries. As my fingers danced upon the keyboard, the imageries became the melody and my writing became the lyrics.

Knowing Jesus as Your Personal Lord & Savior

Many know Jesus as Lord and Savior; but do they know Him as their Lord and Savior? Many believe in God, but even the demons believe and they tremble (James 2:19).

If you do not know Jesus as your Personal Lord and Savior, please receive Him. He waits for you to say, "Yes" today. Remember, tomorrow is not promised. "For today is the day of salvation" (2 Corinthians 6:2).

Jesus gave His life for you; for all of humanity. The Roman soldiers did not take his life; He gave His abundant more than worthy life unto death for God's glory and on our behalf. John 3:16, & 17, the most basic yet powerful scripture which is what we must stand on, "For God so loved the world, that He gave His only begotten Son, that whoever believes in Him should not perish but have everlasting life. For God did not send His Son to condemn the world, but that the world through Him might be saved."

It is amazing to see in verse 16 that God did not just love the world, He so loved the world, with His unfailing love of compassion. I believe He was so saddened by our disconnection from Him, He desires to be reconnected in ways I pray that we experience like never before. So not only did He so love the world, but He also gave His only begotten Son. So, whoever believes in Jesus will not die eternally separated from God in hell, but have everlasting life connected with God.

I believe more than the burning and gnashing of teeth, the overwhelming torment would be to know for eternity our spirit would be separated from God our Father. This is so sad and so hard to comprehend for eternity being separated from God, just imagine how this saddens the Father, for He will not force His will upon ours. I believe He can influence our will through ministering laborers, but He will not change it, He loves us that much to allow us to make our own choices...we either choose Him or we choose the enemy. There is no in between.

So knowing that God gave Jesus and as Jesus ascended into heaven, He promised that the Holy Spirit would come as our Comforter and our strengthener and that we would do things even greater than Jesus did, not by our power or our might but by the power of the Spirit of God (Zechariah 4:6).

I heard it revealed in such a powerful way through a daughter of the King, Lisa Bevere, "Jesus came to reveal the Father and the Holy Spirit has come to reveal the Son, Jesus."

I pray you receive Jesus Christ by faith and receive the baptism of the Holy Spirit. If you are ready please pray this prayer:

"Father God in Jesus Mighty name I receive salvation from my Savior Jesus, for I know He came to earth and lived a victorious life and gave His life unto death and by your resurrection power He was high and lifted up and rose on the third day for those sins I have committed. Thank You

Jesus for coming into my heart and giving me a new life as I receive you. I thank you for Your Holy Spirit baptizing me with power and that I live a life that glorifies You. When I mess up, I will not receive condemnation from my own spirit but will receive the loving conviction of the Holy Spirit and I will repent turning from my wicked ways and follow Your ways. Thank You allowing me to become a new creature for I know that old things have passed away and behold all things become new. Thank you for my new life as You live in me and I live in You. This is the best day of my life for I am reconnected with my Lord and God. Thank You Father for being my Daddy. I pray this prayer by faith in You God, through Jesus powerful name led by God's Holy Spirit. Amen."

Now that you have confessed with your mouth this prayer, I know that you already have a "knowing" within that you are different and are craving for truth, His Word, which is revealed in the person called Jesus. I am so happy for you and I know that heaven celebrates on your behalf as heaven watches in awe that God is glorified by receiving His free gift...His loving gift of Salvation; for He is Salvation.

God bless you as you have read this book. I pray that you are truly blessed and realize the plans that God has for you are for good (Jeremiah 29:11)! God is so great, no matter what the circumstances in life say, He is Continually Awesome!

I love you with the love of God! Be blessed and remember you have an abundant supply from within that is waiting to be poured out onto others for the glory of God!

Love your sister in Christ...Teresa Ann

ABOUT THE AUTHOR

Teresa Ann is the founder and talk show host of, *Triumphant Victorious Reminders with Teresa Ann* via both her podcast and YouTube channels (https://linktr.ee/TriumphantVictorious_Reminders).

She is also an award winning author of several books and the blogs *Triumphant Victorious Reminders* (www.TriumphantVictoriousReminders.com) *The Pee Diaries of A Laughing Mom*, and co-host of the *Oh! Podcast* that she produces with her daughter.

SEVERAL BOOKS TERESA ANN HAS WRITTEN.

Teresa Ann's heart desire is to use every creative tool as a means to point others to the Father God. She enjoys articulating how our lives are to be as a sign, wonder and miracle that points others to the Father GOD as HE "flips the script" in our lives to no longer see from the place of lack but with GOD'S abundant life! If you want this victorious life in Christ, simply ask Jesus Christ to be the Lord of your Life. Let HIM rule your life; go after HIM and watch how your life will forever change. Your life in this temporary world is for the purpose of knowing GOD more so that more people can come to know HIM through your life pointing them to the Father GOD!

If you said, "Yes" to Jesus, who is the ONLY way to GOD, then please contact Teresa Ann via email

LetsTalkTV74@gmail.com

If you enjoyed this book, please leave a review on Amazon and/or Goodreads. Your words will help other readers walk in the truth of God's beauty that HE wants to give to them.

Notes

Notes

Notes

Notes

Notes

Notes

Notes

Notes

Notes

Notes

Notes

Notes

Notes

Notes

Notes

Notes

Notes

Notes

Notes

Notes

Made in the USA
Las Vegas, NV
02 December 2022